Aunts Come Armed with Welsh Cakes
Thirza Clout

smith|doorstop

Published 2019 by
Smith|Doorstop Books
The Poetry Business
Campo House
54 Campo Lane
Sheffield S1 2EG

Copyright © Thirza Clout 2019
All Rights Reserved
ISBN 978-1-912196-67-8

Designed and Typeset by Utter
Printed by Biddles Books

Acknowledgements
'what you would not want discovered after you die' was first published by *Banshee Literary Magazine*; along with 'the streets are full' it was also included in the *Wolf Hoard* anthology published (Border Poets, 2018). The first line of 'legacy' is from 'When I am dead, my dearest' by Christina Rossetti.

Smith|Doorstop Books are a member of Inpress: www.inpressbooks.co.uk. Distributed by NBN International, Airport Business Centre, 10 Thornbury Road Plymouth PL6 7PP

The Poetry Business gratefully acknowledges the support of Arts Council England.

Contents

5	Breech
6	Music
7	Cousin Monica
8	Thirza
9	Aunts
10	Treat
11	All Souls' Night
12	A Present
13	Dan
14	January
15	girls
16	albums
17	telling
18	I am so sick of watching women die
19	Henrik had so much to say at book group
20	In Shropshire
21	The Bitterley Hoard
22	forty years
24	intimacy
25	legacy
26	Carpe diem
27	what you would not want discovered after you die
28	the streets are full
30	Honey

*To Anna Dreda, founder of Wenlock Poetry Festival
and a true friend to poetry and poets.*

Breech

Twice she caught buses twenty miles to hospital
two hours each way with three changes
waiting on swollen feet at stops without seats
standing heavily in the heat of that July,
endured gloved invasions to swim me round.
She told anyone how quickly I flipped back
kicking her womb as she carried her burdens home.
Especially she loved to emphasise how her waters broke
while she was serving groceries in the village shop.
Contrary from the start, that was her punchline.

I turned myself around to leave – headfirst I pushed
away from her. With her thumbprint she signed my navel
tenderly she pleated my newborn skin
taped on an old penny to mend the umbilical hernia.

Music

I worshipped my big brother when he played double bass
plucking skiffle from brown string tied to a broomstick
putting on the style. Mother said *that boy could fall
into a cesspit and come up with a new hat on.*

She longed for his visits, went away to nurse his wife
although I was sick. Clearing her house I found
she kept his postcards tied with ribbon.
In secret I burned all his distant news
scribbled in writing formed far too like my own.

Cousin Monica

Smoke rises into damp air at Pontypool Crem
as we park and try to recognise each other.
We don't mention her lung cancer or ask her kids
and almost adult grandkids to stub out their cigs.

Standing guard at the door her younger brother Dai,
dark suit failing to contain him and his grief, flails a punch
at Monica's son Dewi Bach, reconciled to her
beside the hospital bed but here still unforgiven.

Looking away the rest of us file in. Out of tune we cannot
scale 'Abide With Me' nor banish 'Death's Dark Vale'.
Amid our straining discords I think of Mon,
mourn our silence, wish we had sung out together
those family secrets I suspect we shared
sung them out loud then cast them to the flames.

Thirza

She stood tall, a fierce woman whose mouth
sparked hot as Blaenavon furnaces, her heart
deep as Crumlin colliery, her big hands never
stopped working nor stirring. Thirza's son-in-law,
such an angry little drinker who starved his wife
knocked out her teeth and beat their baby,
he drowned in the reservoir close by Thirza's house.
Death by misadventure the coroner said.

Aunty Thirza baked the best Welsh cakes I'll ever eat
the secret was lard, she said butter was for lah-di-dahs.
She worked three cleaning jobs, ran a launderette,
kept a scrubbed-up voice for best which made me laugh
until she turned it on me, poured out molten iron:
the bosses are in charge my girl and don't you forget it.

Aunts

Our family was lopsided, buoyed up on the bosoms
of plentiful aunts but near capsizing with such a weight
on Dad's side. Edie, Thirza, Ivy, Hilda nicknamed Hobbs
for her childhood crush on the cricketer, all were his sisters.

Glamorous Agnes whose beginnings Mother called bog-Irish,
poor put-upon Nelly who died young, his sisters-in-law;
Great Aunt Lizzie, who was very particular, was his Mam's sister.
Mother had two distant cousins she seldom saw.

Visiting aunts came armed with Welsh cakes, great tins full
(sugar, lard, flour, generous quantities of currants,
milk and egg to bind them, then browned on the bakestone).
A needy child I counted sleeps, longing for their arrival.

One time I saw my mother weeping on Thirza's shoulder
once overheard mother accusing all the aunts
of ruining me with too much love – her own legacy
she passed on: *spare the rod and spoil the child.*

She did not speak of the never-aunts Joan and Mary
whose infant deaths had left her an only child
nursing her parents cursing through old age. Henry
stumbling on crutches hobbled by arthritis and strong

Kent barley wine, blind Maud ten times hourly asking mother
to untangle her unfinished knitting, lead her to the outdoor privy.
Maud disappeared into the County Lunatic Asylum when I was five
I don't remember that anyone ever said to me how or when she died.

Treat

When Dad thickly buttered
a slice of white bread, spooned

on sugar, tipped it to and fro
over the china bowl

he showered down so much love
it snowed across the cloth.

I licked my first finger, pressed down
to stick grains, licked again.

In our house love came granulated
never enough to be wasted.

All Souls' Night

Last time Mum and Dad visited me
they were both long dead, she
for a decade, he thirty years or more.

Mum wore her warm checked coat,
Dad was in Sunday best, white shirt
pressed, no tie, his hair still red. I
poured tea into their bone china cups

said I'd bake Welsh cakes in no time at all
but they weren't stopping. They just called
to kiss me and to give me words of love,
words I'd never heard in all the years before.

Through the thirty nights of November
I longed to welcome them again. The cakes
went mouldy in the tin, the kettle was cold.

A Present

The last gift my mother gave me
was her death

she did not linger at the threshold
wait six months to celebrate

eighty years. Resolute, she turned
her slumped face towards the wall

willed a final stroke. As she could not speak
I voiced her wishes, refused antibiotics

told her absent son and other daughter
she is not in pain. I did not tell them

that when a fire alarm rang
suddenly her eyes opened wide.

Paralysed and speechless perhaps she dreamt
she would be burned alive.

I held her hand tightly
said I would never leave her

later understood that was the opposite
of what she wanted me to do.

Dan

Beyond a double row of Bramley trees
past the glasshouse where in winter
dahlias sleep tucked into peat, he is digging,
pausing, looking at every spadeful
stooping to pick out groundsel
chickweed, couch grass roots.

He hears birds easily singing, no need for him
to stutter a reply. Robins fight for their ground,
blackbirds and bullfinches eat grubs, peck buds,
wary eyes cocked for his ginger cat.
Indoors and out Dan wears a checked cap
adds a shocking red scarf from first frost to last.

He gathers apples and pears, sells baskets of cobnuts,
picks freesias, pink lilies, frothing gypsophilia,
flowers for other men's brides to carry.
He culls stiff sprays of chrysanthemums,
white arums and laurel to weave into wreaths
for the dead in his village who have families to grieve.

January

not in a kiss-arse every sock gives me joy kind of way
not in a tidy house tidy mind smug-arse kind of way
not in a bloodless tight-arse minimalist kind of way
this is the year I declutter in a bad-arse kind of way

this is the year I rip out the guts from ancient carcasses
kept mouldering too long in the dark under my bed
this is the year I smash every cup and saucer Granny left
just as cracked and crazed as she was at her end
burn unread all the letters from my father my mother kept
blaze them on a bonfire – watch them vanish into warmed air.

girls

what would we have without naughty girls
mouthy girls, bolshie girls, girls who won't fit in
all those girls who don't give up
won't shut up when men talk across them
who take risks and raise their voices
won't be shouted down or bantered out of it

we good girls are silenced when we are groped
silenced when we are passed over
silenced when we are paid less
good girls play the game believing we will be rewarded
and so we always are with sweet fuck all

it takes girls who are called strident girls called sluts
girls who delete the tweeted threats and face down the trolling
girls who go beyond the pale to change the world

albums

camouflage creeps up on you

at five minus two front teeth
you face the camera smiling

by nine your face lies
behind shadows

at eleven you turn away
buttons straining on your blouse

in your teens you plunge into cover
hair curtains your feelings

nobody loves a smartarse
you turn down your wattage

too many years later
you throw your fatigues on the floor

at last turn up the lights

telling

details burn
the tongue-red lid
of a Brylcreem jar
lolling on his dressing table
must be tidied away

you want me to chat to him
eat slices of wedding
and birthday cakes
at family funerals see me
swallow my rage

I am so sick of watching women die

I want Mimi to buy herself a pair of gloves
to warm her tiny frozen hands

I want Odette to kick Siegfried in the nuts
to break the stupid spell

I want Ophelia to jilt Hamlet and rule Denmark
after all the men finish killing each other

I want Hedda to get a job and enjoy multiple orgasms
with lots of lovers who are good to her

I want Emma to get an education and discover
marriage and poison are not her only options

I want Olga, Masha and Irina to laugh
and conquer Moscow – and Anna simply must

get custody of her son, ditch Vronsky
and join the Three Sisters' book group

I want to see living on stage and screen and page
women working, loving, women surviving

Henrik had so much to say at book group

He was fascinating about the female psyche,
his understanding of our tendency to self-destruct
was immense and he is modestly pleased to remain
the go-to playwright on women's issues for so long

after his death. He claimed but a tiny credit for female suffrage
warmly encouraged us to work harder to achieve equal pay.
Centre stage, Hedda remained silent for an hour
then jumped up and threw her wine in his face. Nora

laughed loudly and left – she slammed the door before
Henrik explained how hysteria would destroy them both.
As one book group we rose up to stuff his mouth with hummus
above his smothered cries we shouted: *shut up and listen to us.*

In Shropshire

snowdrops drift under the yews
beside the metal plaque on the churchyard wall
marking high tide from the Great Flood
of 1684

sometimes they wash up next to it
two brothers staring

the chestnut tree is flexing thin new stems
from a stump left after it crushed
a car a while ago – that was one time
they weren't standing there
watching everything
not happening here.

The Bitterley Hoard

The farmer knows his land, thinks where soil is softest
in-bye pasture, the far ditch corner between two elms.
Behind closed shutters he listens to the night, his wife stirs
turns over, breathes evenly again. He takes the small brown tyg
fills it to the brim but not with drink, instead he pushes in
his leather purse stacked with coin. He creeps out, pads across the mud
pulls his shovel from the midden heap, hears a rustle, strains his eyes
catches the shadow of the old dog fox as it fades into the hedge.
He digs, lays down the tyg, covers it over, careful to leave no trace.
Satisfied he swills soil from his hands, joins his wife in sleep.

His treasure survives civil war and centuries of tilling, ploughs
broke off shards but still the tyg holds the purse, calf-skin soft,
his coins still safe. Hedge, ditch and farmhouse are faint lines
across the landscape; the farmer and the fox have gone to earth.

forty years

I love the way you take such pains
to mend broken things
apply superglue to fractured joints
handles of mugs we loved
cracked vases and jugs

you wash common geranium roots
free them from convolvulus
handle them tenderly as limbs
of the newborn babies
we could not have

forty years ago I loved the way
you never wanted to change your car
didn't care if moss
mottled the bonnet
passion stained the seats

I love the way we have transformed
blank space and concrete
a riot of roses scents the air
above tangles of nettles
rampaging ground elder

I love the pond we made crowded with newts
blue and yellow flags of iris, azure damsels
red darters, big striped dragonflies
helicoptering above water lilies
black cats pouncing from the shadows

in summer evenings we drank wine
listening to hooligan swifts, glimpsing bats
hunting from the church tower, breathing in
honeysuckle grown from cuttings leapfrogged
from Cornwall to Somerset to Shropshire

home from winter walks we shiver
turn away from our graveyard neighbours
stir up the fires to keep out frosts

intimacy

you lie beside me locked in sleep

as always we kissed
before you put out your light
curved away and
huddled under covers

when I turn pages
more noisily than I meant
you stir and murmur words
I cannot quite

we talk of dreams
you never tell
what mares gallop by.

legacy

when I am dead my dearest
I wish you shooting stars

from our honeymoon I wish you
kingfishers and mating fireflies

from the steep lanes cradling Luppitt
I wish you humble glow-worms

from the garden we have made
I wish you roses, jasmine and potatoes

pink fir apples, waxy charlottes
rainbow chard and bountiful runner beans

Carpe diem

I have had so many tomorrows after so many nights before
good nights, daft nights, quarrel and fight nights,
nights when I have had my drinking boots on,
not much else by the end of those nights.

Gin and tonic nights, white wine and red nights
any port in a storm – call me a taxi but not quite yet nights,
too many tomorrows with my clothes tossed aside
as twilight fades around the edges of the wrong blind.

Tonight though, this is a night to party party party, tonight
I cannot stop to reckon how many tomorrows might remain.

what you would not want discovered after you die

includes the chaos of your sock drawer
thick woollen walkers jostling tights
both sheer and laddered – pop socks

you do not want to die wearing pop socks

every time you tug the drawer open
one hand shoving stuff flatter
odd socks tired of waiting years
for perfect matches
discard themselves upon the floor
you blow the dust off them before
you restore them to disorder

includes the faux leather basque
and anything else from Ann Summers
even if the batteries are flat

includes the little box containing
a dozen perfectly ironed handkerchiefs
with your mother's initials

includes the knowledge that this is the only thing
you kept from her pin-neat drawers

– blouses folded, tea towels ironed, socks paired –

the only thing you didn't stuff
into the black plastic bin bags.

the streets are full

of slender people
body-con T-shirts
tucked
into belts
skinny jeans

they are laughing
sipping
skinny lattes
nibbling
pomegranate
seeds

they move
easily
along
narrow
pavements
cleared of fat
people

all we fat people are sitting at home
expecting a caller who will point a bony finger
expecting a caller who will tell us we are weighing down the world
a caller who will tell us we are time bombs of flesh primed to destroy the NHS
clinically obese guerrillas armed with knives and forks and spoons

we will put down our crisps and biscuits, our glasses of wine
lay down our diet books, our sugar-free colas and low-cal snacks
obediently we will follow the skeleton in the black hoodie

some of us are hoping he leads us to a promised land
all of us expect it will be filled with milk and honey

Honey

Who is the man feeding me honey made by birds?
In his square hands he holds a conical nest
shifting clouds of blue tiny birds
halo his head. I dip a teaspoon
into the dark clear honey made by birds
and sip. Smiling he invites me to lick
a wooden spurtle, lap up the honey made by birds.

It tastes of the pure white columns of birch trees.
I am astonished: there is honey made by birds,
in this world I know the taste of birch trees.